A Yard for All

By D.M. Longo

Illustrated by Jackie Snider

Target Skill Realism and Fantasy

PEARSON

Scott
Foresman

He is buzzing!
It is his yard.

The rabbit is hopping!
It is his yard.

The fish is swimming!
It is her yard.

The bug is jumping.
It is her yard.

The dogs are digging.
It is their yard.

The birds are resting.
It is their yard.

It is a yard for all!